BLUES PLAY-ALONG

Book & CD for B♭, E♭, Bass Clef and C instruments

VOLUME 15

BLUES Ballads

PLAY 8 SONGS WITH A PROFESSIONAL BAND

HOW TO USE THE CD:

Each song has two tracks:

1) Full Stereo Mix

All recorded instruments are present on this track.

2) Split Track

Piano and **Bass** parts can be removed
by turning down the volume on the LEFT channel.

Guitar and **Horn** parts can be removed
by turning down the volume on the RIGHT channel.

ISBN 978-1-4234-9654-0

HAL•LEONARD® CORPORATION

7777 W. BLUEMOUND RD. P.O. BOX 13819 MILWAUKEE, WI 53213

Visit Hal Leonard Online at
www.halleonard.com

Ain't No Sunshine
Words and Music by Bill Withers

Intro
Moderately slow ♩ = 78

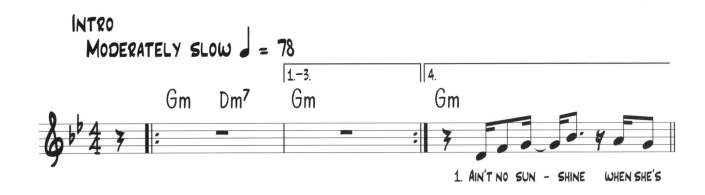

1. Ain't no sun - shine when she's

VERSE

GONE.
2. See additional lyrics

It's not warm ___ when ___ she's a -

WAY.

Ain't no sun - shine ___ when she's

GONE. ___ She's al - ways gone ___ too long an - y - time she goes a -

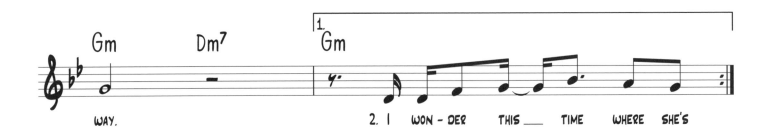

WAY.

2. I won - der this ___ time where she's

I KNOW, I KNOW, I KNOW, _____

I KNOW, I KNOW, I KNOW, _____   I KNOW, I KNOW, I KNOW, ____

I KNOW, I KNOW, I KNOW, ____   I OUGHT TO LEAVE THE YOUNG THING A - LONE _ 'CAUSE AIN'T NO SUN-

- SHINE _____   WHEN SHE'S   GONE. _____

3. AIN'T NO SUN - SHINE   WHEN SHE'S   GONE.
4. SEE ADDITIONAL LYRICS

ON - LY DARK - NESS   EV - 'RY   DAY.

AIN'T NO SUN - SHINE ____ WHEN SHE'S   GONE, ___   SHE'S AL - WAYS GONE __ TOO

LONG AN - Y - TIME SHE GOES A - WAY.

SOLOS

OUTRO
w/Voc. ad lib. on repeats

⊕ CODA

AN - Y - TIME ___ SHE GOES A - WAY.

AN - Y - TIME ___ SHE GOES A -

ADDITIONAL LYRICS

2. I wonder this time where she's gone,
   I wonder if she's gone to stay.
   Ain't no sunshine when she's gone,
   And this house just ain't no home.
   Anytime she goes away.

4. It's not warm when she's away,
   Only darkness every day.
   Ain't no sunshine when she's gone,
   She's always gone too long,
   Anytime she goes away.

Have You Ever Loved a Woman

Words and Music by Billy Myles

%: VERSE

Moderately slow ♩. = 64

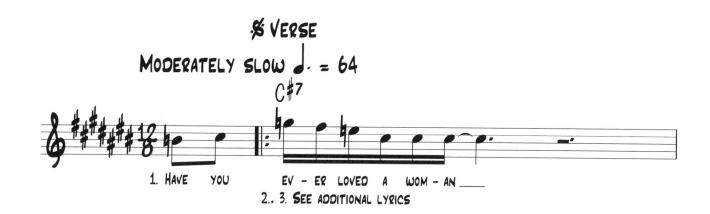

1. Have you ev - er loved a wom - an ___
2., 3. See additional lyrics

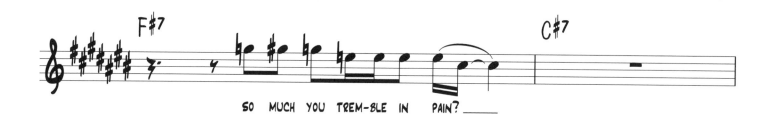

so much you trem-ble in pain? ___

Yes, ___ have you ev-er loved ___ a wom-an ___

so ___ much ___ you trem-ble in ___ pain? ___

3rd time, To Coda ⊕

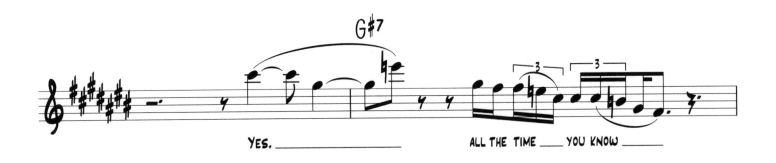

YES. _____ ALL THE TIME ___ YOU KNOW _____

SHE ___ BEARS ___ AN-OTH-ER ___ MAN'S _____ NAME. _____

2. YOU JUST

SOLOS

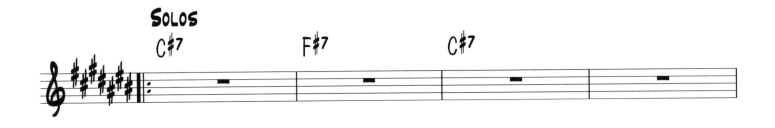

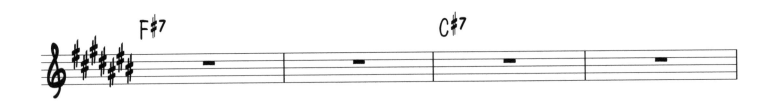

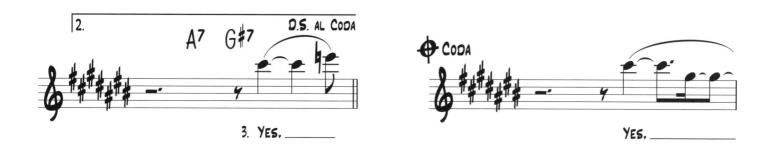

3. YES, ____

Ⓞ CODA

YES, ____

____ 'CAUSE THERE'S SOME-THING DEEP IN-SIDE OF YOU, ____

WON'T LET YOU WRECK YOUR BEST FRIEND'S _ HOME. ____

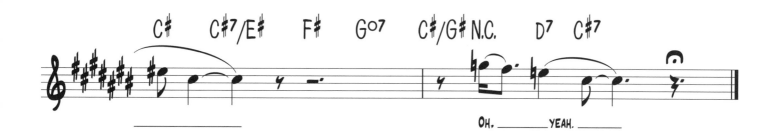

____ OH, ____ YEAH. ____

ADDITIONAL LYRICS

2. YOU JUST LOVE THAT WOMAN SO MUCH IT'S A SHAME AND A SIN.
   YES, YOU JUST LOVE THAT WOMAN SO MUCH IT'S A SHAME AND A SIN.
   YES, YOU KNOW, YES, YOU KNOW SHE BELONGS TO YOUR VERY BEST FRIEND.

3. YES, HAVE YOU EVERE LOVED A WOMAN, ONE THAT YOU KNOW YOU CAN'T LEAVE ALONE?
   YES, HAVE YOU EVERE LOVED A WOMAN, YEAH, ONE THAT YOU KNOW YOU CAN'T LEAVE ALONE?
   YES, 'CAUSE THERE'S SOMETHING DEEP INSIDE OF YOU, WON'T LET YOU WRECK YOUR BEST FRIEND'S HOME.

As the Years Go Passing By

Words and Music by Deadric Malone

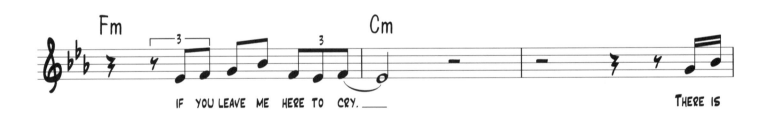

ADDITIONAL LYRICS

2. I GIVE YOU ALL I OWN; THAT'S ONE THING YOU CAN'T DENY.
   YEAH, I GIVE YOU ALL I OWN; YOU KNOW THAT'S ONE THING YOU CAN'T DENY.
   YES, MY LOVE WILL FOLLOW YOU AS THE YEARS GO PASSING BY.

3. I'M GONNA LEAVE IT UP TO YOU. SO LONG, SO LONG GOODBYE.
   I'M GONNA LEAVE IT UP TO YOU. SO LONG, SO LONG GOODBYE.
   YOU KNOW, MY LOVE WILL FOLLOW YOU AS THE YEARS GO PASSING BY.

DARLIN' YOU KNOW I LOVE YOU

WORDS AND MUSIC BY B.B. KING AND JULES BIHARI

Additional Lyrics

2. I think of you ev'ry morning
   And dream of you ev'ry night.
   And I would love to be with you always.

3. Oh, darlin', you know I love you
   And love you by myself,
   But you've gone and left me for someone else.

I'd Rather Go Blind

Words and Music by Ellington Jordan and Billy Foster

Most of all I just don't, I just don't wan-na be free,__ Lord.

I was just,__ I was just,_____ I was just__ sit-tin' here think-in'_____

of your kiss and your warm em - brace,__ yeah,

when the re-flec - tion in the glass__ that I held____ to my lips, now, babe,__

re-vealed the tears that was on_____ my face._____

Chorus

And ba - by, ba - by____ I'd rath-er, I'd rath-er be blind,__ boy,__

than to see you walk a-way, see you walk a-way from me,____ yeah.

Outro-Solos

1.

2.

SOMEBODY LOAN ME A DIME

WORDS AND MUSIC BY FENTON ROBINSON

INTRO
MODERATELY SLOW ♩ = 76

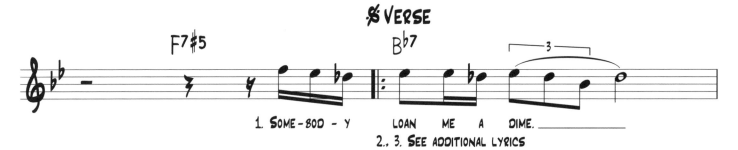

1. SOME-BOD-Y LOAN ME A DIME. ___
2., 3. SEE ADDITIONAL LYRICS

I WAN-NA CALL ___ MY OLD-TIME USED TO BE. ___

SOME-BOD-Y LOAN ME A DIME ___ I TELL YOU. ___

I WAN-NA CALL MY OLD-TIME USED TO BE. ___

YOU KNOW THE WOM-AN SHE BEEN GONE SO LONG. ___

ADDITIONAL LYRICS

2. Now, I just cry, I just cry, I cry like a baby all night long.
   Oh, how I cry, how I cry, I cry like a baby all night long.
   But oh, I need somebody, I need somebody here in my home.

3. And now I know she's a good girl, but at that time I just didn't understand.
   Oh, I know, I know she's a good girl, but at that time I just didn't understand.
   But oh, somebody loan me a dime, just to ease my worried mind.

Third Degree

Written by Willie Dixon and Eddie Boyd

Intro
Slow ♩ = 50

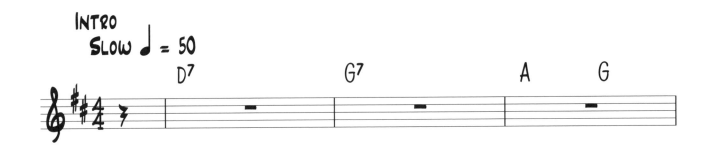

% Verse

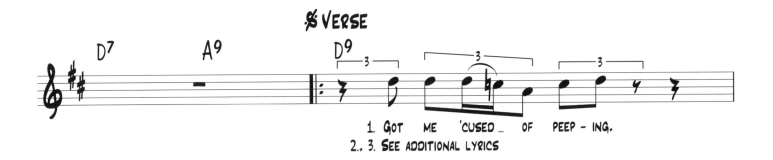

1. Got me 'cused of peep-ing.
2., 3. See additional lyrics

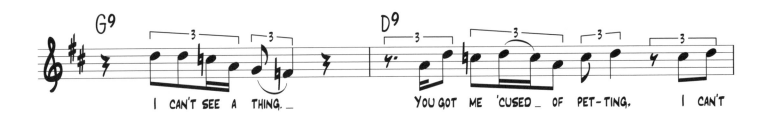

I can't see a thing. ___   You got me 'cused of pet-ting,   I can't

E - ven raise my hand. _____   Bad   luck. _____

Bad ___ luck is kill-in' me.   Now, I

JUST ___ CAN'T STAND ___ NO MORE ___ OF THIS THIRD DE -

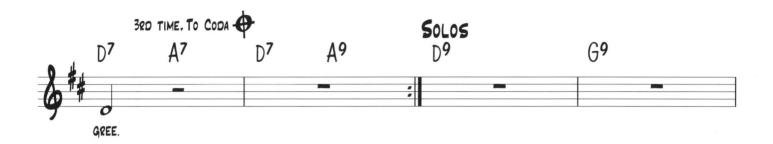

3RD TIME, TO CODA ⊕

SOLOS

GREE.

D.S. AL CODA

⊕ CODA

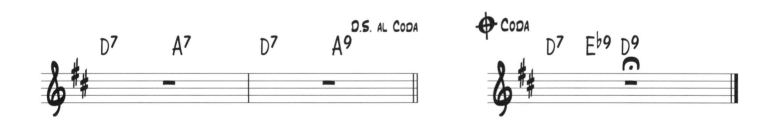

ADDITIONAL LYRICS

2. GOT ME 'CUSED OF MURDER, I'VE NEVER HARMED A MAN.
YOU GOT ME 'CUSED OF FORGERY, I CAN'T EVEN WRITE MY NAME.
BAD LUCK, BAD LUCK IS KILLIN' ME.
NOW, I JUST CAN'T STAND NO MORE OF THIS THIRD DEGREE.

3. GOT ME 'CUSED OF TAXES, I DON'T HAVE A LOUSY DIME.
YOU GOT ME 'CUSED OF CHILDREN, AIN'T NARY ONE OF THEM MINE.
BAD LUCK, BAD LUCK IS KILLIN' ME.
NOW, I JUST CAN'T STAND NO MORE OF THIS THIRD DEGREE.

Three Hours Past Midnight

Words and Music by Johnny Watson and Saul Bihari

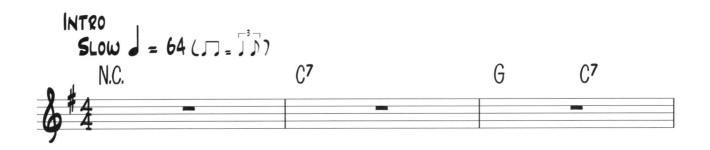

Intro
Slow ♩ = 64

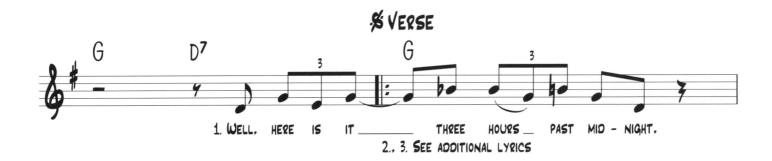

♪ Verse

1. Well, here is it _____ three hours _ past mid - night,
2., 3. See additional lyrics

and my _____ ba - by's _____ no - where a - round. _____

Well, here it is _____ three hours _ past mid - night.

and my ba - by's ___ no - where a - round. _____ Well, I

Additional Lyrics

2. Yes, I tossed and tumbled on my pillow, but I just can't close my eyes.
   Yes, I tossed and tumbled on my pillow, and I just can't close my eyes.
   If my baby don't come back pretty quick,
   Yes, I just can't be satisfied.

3. Well, I want my baby, I want her by my side.
   Well, I want my baby, yes, I want her by my side.
   Well, and if she don't come home pretty soon,
   Yes, I just can't be satisfied.

Ain't No Sunshine

Words and Music by Bill Withers

Intro
Moderately slow ♩ = 78

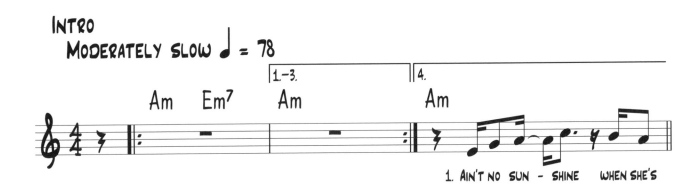

Am   Em⁷ |1.–3. Am |4. Am

1. Ain't no sun - shine when she's

Verse

Am   Em⁷   Am

gone.
2. See additional lyrics

It's not warm ___ when ___ she's a –

Em⁷   Am

way.

Ain't no sun - shine ___ when she's

Em⁷   Dm⁷

gone. ___ She's al - ways gone ___ too long   an - y - time she goes a –

Am   Em⁷ |1. Am

way.

2. I won - der this ___ time where she's

2.
Am

§ BRIDGE
N.C.

I KNOW, I KNOW, I KNOW, ____

I KNOW, I KNOW, I KNOW, ____   I KNOW, I KNOW, I KNOW, ____

I KNOW, I KNOW, I KNOW, ____   I OUGHT TO LEAVE THE YOUNG THING A-LONE _ 'CAUSE AIN'T NO SUN-

Am   Em⁷

- SHINE ____   WHEN SHE'S GONE. ____

VERSE
Am   Em⁷

Am

3. AIN'T NO SUN-SHINE   WHEN SHE'S   GONE.
4. SEE ADDITIONAL LYRICS

Am   Em⁷

ON-LY DARK-NESS   EV-'RY DAY.

Am   Em⁷

AIN'T NO SUN-SHINE ____ WHEN SHE'S GONE, ____ SHE'S AL-WAYS GONE ____ TOO

23

Additional Lyrics

2. I wonder this time where she's gone,
I wonder if she's gone to stay.
Ain't no sunshine when she's gone,
And this house just ain't no home.
Anytime she goes away.

4. It's not warm when she's away,
Only darkness every day.
Ain't no sunshine when she's gone,
She's always gone too long,
Anytime she goes away.

Have You Ever Loved a Woman

Words and Music by Billy Myles

% VERSE

Moderately slow ♩. = 64

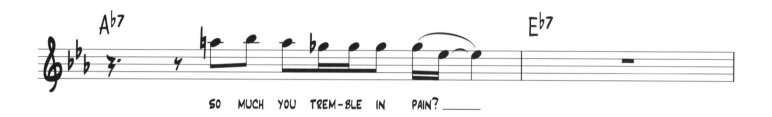

1. Have you ev-er loved a wom-an ____
2., 3. See additional lyrics

so much you trem-ble in pain? ____

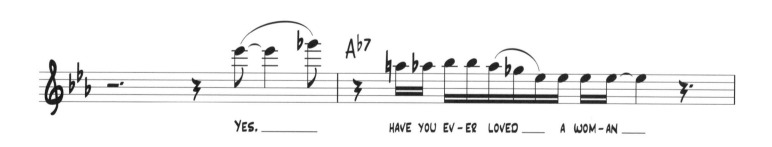

Yes, ____ have you ev-er loved ____ a wom-an ____

so ____ much ____ you trem-ble in ____ pain? ____

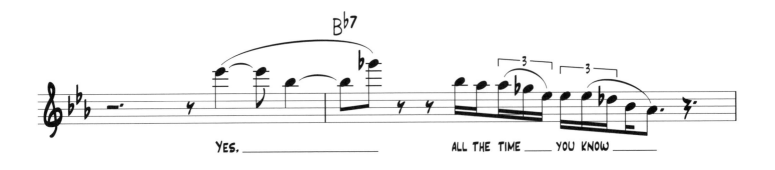

YES, _____ ALL THE TIME ____ YOU KNOW ____

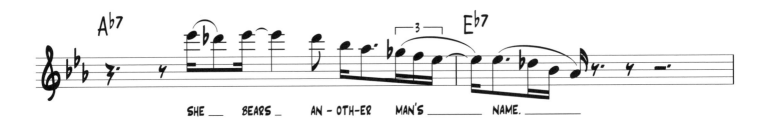

SHE __ BEARS _ AN-OTH-ER MAN'S _____ NAME. ____

2. YOU JUST

SOLOS

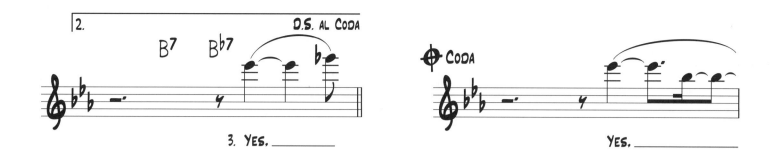

3. YES, _____

YES, _____

'CAUSE THERE'S SOME-THING DEEP IN-SIDE OF YOU, _____

WON'T LET YOU WRECK YOUR BEST FRIEND'S _ HOME. _____

OH, _____ YEAH. _____

ADDITIONAL LYRICS

2. YOU JUST LOVE THAT WOMAN SO MUCH IT'S A SHAME AND A SIN.
   YES, YOU JUST LOVE THAT WOMAN SO MUCH IT'S A SHAME AND A SIN.
   YES, YOU KNOW, YES, YOU KNOW SHE BELONGS TO YOUR VERY BEST FRIEND.

3. YES, HAVE YOU EVERE LOVED A WOMAN, ONE THAT YOU KNOW YOU CAN'T LEAVE ALONE?
   YES, HAVE YOU EVERE LOVED A WOMAN, YEAH, ONE THAT YOU KNOW YOU CAN'T LEAVE ALONE?
   YES, 'CAUSE THERE'S SOMETHING DEEP INSIDE OF YOU, WON'T LET YOU WRECK YOUR BEST FRIEND'S HOME.

As the Years Go Passing By

Words and Music by Deadric Malone

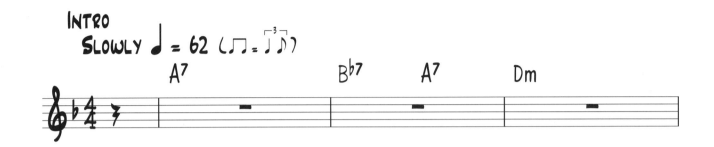

INTRO
SLOWLY ♩ = 62

Additional Lyrics

2. I give you all I own; that's one thing you can't deny.
   Yeah, I give you all I own; you know that's one thing you can't deny.
   Yes, my love will follow you as the years go passing by.

3. I'm gonna leave it up to you. So long, so long goodbye.
   I'm gonna leave it up to you. So long, so long goodbye.
   You know, my love will follow you as the years go passing by.

Darlin' You Know
I Love You

Words and Music by B.B. King and Jules Bihari

HOLD YOU IN MY ARMS TO - NIGHT. 3. OH,___

SOLOS

OH, DAR - LIN', YOU KNOW I ___ LOVE YOU AND ___

LOVE YOU BY ___ MY - SELF, BUT YOU'VE GONE _____ AND

LEFT ME, BA - BY, ___ FOR SOME - ONE ELSE. _____

ADDITIONAL LYRICS

2. I THINK OF YOU EV'RY MORNING
   AND DREAM OF YOU EV'RY NIGHT.
   AND I WOULD LOVE TO BE WITH YOU ALWAYS.

3. OH, DARLIN', YOU KNOW I LOVE YOU
   AND LOVE YOU BY MYSELF,
   BUT YOU'VE GONE AND LEFT ME FOR SOMEONE ELSE.

I'd Rather Go Blind
Words and Music by Ellington Jordan and Billy Foster

Intro
Slow ♩. = 55

Verse

1. Some-thing told __ me it was o - ver when I saw __ you __ and her talk-ing. __ Some-thing deep down in my soul __ said,"Cry, __ girl." __ when I saw you __ and that girl __ walk- ing. __ now.

Chorus

I would rath-er, I would rath-er go blind. __ Boy, __ than to see you walk a - way __ from me, child. ____ 2. Oo, __

Verse

So you see, I love you so much that I don't wan-na watch you leave me, ba - by.

Most of all I just don't, I just don't wan-na be free.__ Lord.

I was just,__ I was just,____ I was just__ sit-tin' here think-in'____

of your kiss and your warm em - brace,__ yeah.

when the re-flec - tion in the glass __ that I held __ to my lips, now, babe,__

re-vealed the tears that was on ____ my face.____

Chorus

And ba-by, ba-by ___ I'd rath-er, I'd rath-er be blind,__ boy,__

than to see you walk a-way, see you walk a-way from me,___ yeah.

Outro-Solos

Somebody Loan Me a Dime

Words and Music by Fenton Robinson

Intro
Moderately slow ♩ = 76

%‌ Verse

1. Some-bod-y loan me a dime. _____
2., 3. See additional lyrics

I wan-na call _____ my old-time used to be. _____

Some-bod-y loan me a dime _____ I tell you. _____

I wan-na call my old-time used to be. _____

3rd Time, To Coda ⊕

You know the wom-an she been gone so long. _____

ADDITIONAL LYRICS

2. Now, I just cry, I just cry, I cry like a baby all night long.
   Oh, how I cry, how I cry, I cry like a baby all night long.
   But oh, I need somebody, I need somebody here in my home.

3. And now I know she's a good girl, but at that time I just didn't understand.
   Oh, I know, I know she's a good girl, but at that time I just didn't understand.
   But oh, somebody loan me a dime, just to ease my worried mind.

Third Degree
Written by Willie Dixon and Eddie Boyd

INTRO
Slow ♩ = 50

1. Got me 'cused of peep-ing,
2., 3. See additional lyrics

I can't see a thing. ___ You got me 'cused of pet-ting, I can't

E - ven raise my hand. _____ Bad luck. _____

Bad ___ luck is kill-in' me. Now, I

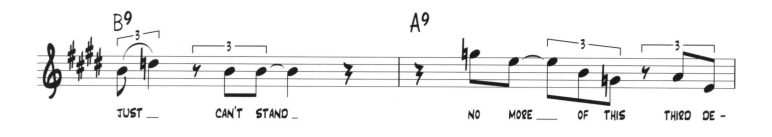

JUST __ CAN'T STAND __ NO MORE __ OF THIS THIRD DE -

3RD TIME, TO CODA 🎯

SOLOS

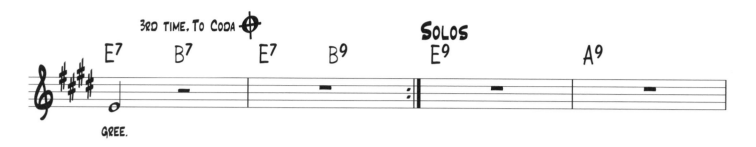

GREE.

D.S. AL CODA

🎯 CODA

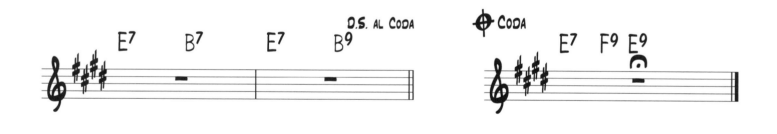

ADDITIONAL LYRICS

2. GOT ME 'CUSED OF MURDER, I'VE NEVER HARMED A MAN.
   YOU GOT ME 'CUSED OF FORGERY, I CAN'T EVEN WRITE MY NAME.
   BAD LUCK, BAD LUCK IS KILLIN' ME.
   NOW, I JUST CAN'T STAND NO MORE OF THIS THIRD DEGREE.

3. GOT ME 'CUSED OF TAXES, I DON'T HAVE A LOUSY DIME.
   YOU GOT ME 'CUSED OF CHILDREN, AIN'T NARY ONE OF THEM MINE.
   BAD LUCK, BAD LUCK IS KILLIN' ME.
   NOW, I JUST CAN'T STAND NO MORE OF THIS THIRD DEGREE.

Three Hours Past Midnight

Words and Music by Johnny Watson and Saul Bihari

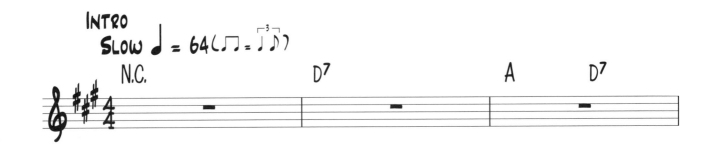

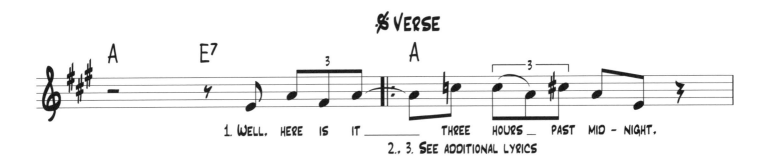

1. Well, here is it _____ three hours _ past mid - night.
2., 3. See additional lyrics

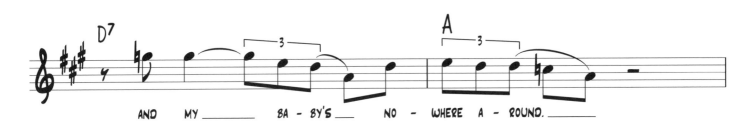

and my _____ ba - by's _ no - where a - round. _____

Well, here it is _____ three hours _ past mid - night.

and my ba - by's _ no - where a - round. _____ Well, I

Additional Lyrics

2. Yes, I tossed and tumbled on my pillow, but I just can't close my eyes.
Yes, I tossed and tumbled on my pillow, and I just can't close my eyes.
If my baby don't come back pretty quick,
Yes, I just can't be satisfied.

3. Well, I want my baby, I want her by my side.
Well, I want my baby, yes, I want her by my side.
Well, and if she don't come home pretty soon,
Yes, I just can't be satisfied.

Ain't No Sunshine

Words and Music by Bill Withers

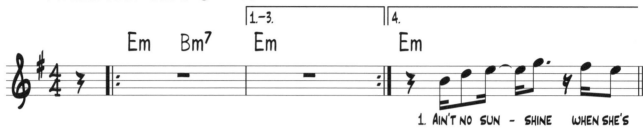

INTRO
MODERATELY SLOW ♩ = 78

1. Ain't no sun - shine when she's

VERSE

gone. It's not warm __ when __ she's a -
2. See additional lyrics

way. Ain't no sun - shine __ when she's

gone. __ She's al - ways gone __ too long an - y - time she goes a -

way. 2. I won - der this __ time where she's

LONG AN - Y - TIME SHE GOES A - WAY.

Solos

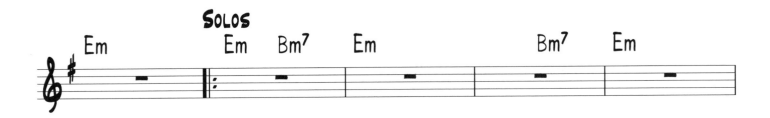

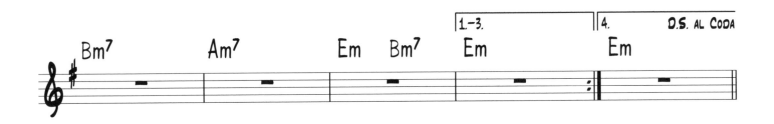

Coda

Outro
w/Voc. ad lib. on repeats

AN - Y - TIME ___ SHE GOES A - WAY.

AN - Y - TIME ___ SHE GOES A -

Additional Lyrics

2. I wonder this time where she's gone.
   I wonder if she's gone to stay.
   Ain't no sunshine when she's gone,
   And this house just ain't no home.
   Anytime she goes away.

4. It's not warm when she's away,
   Only darkness every day.
   Ain't no sunshine when she's gone,
   She's always gone too long,
   Anytime she goes away.

Have You Ever Loved a Woman

Words and Music by Billy Myles

%· Verse

Moderately slow ♩· = 64

1. Have you ev-er loved a wom-an ____

2., 3. See additional lyrics

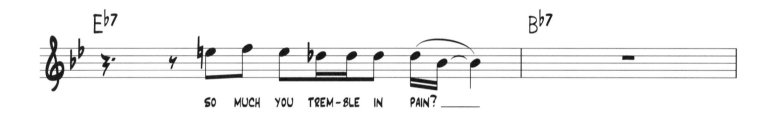

So much you trem-ble in pain? ____

Yes, ____ have you ev-er loved ____ a wom-an ____

3rd time, To Coda ⊕

So ____ much ____ you trem-ble in ____ pain? ____

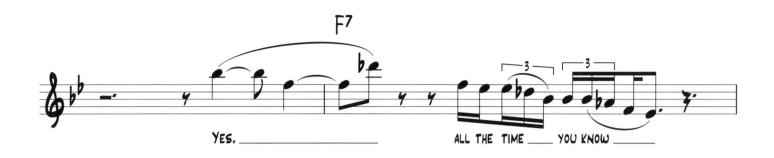

YES, _____ ALL THE TIME _____ YOU KNOW _____

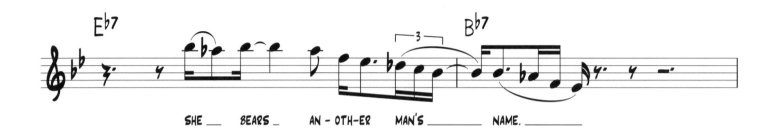

SHE _____ BEARS _____ AN - OTH-ER _____ MAN'S _____ NAME. _____

2. YOU JUST

SOLOS

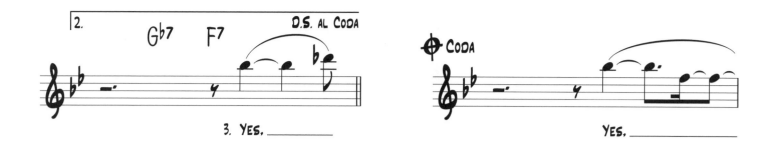

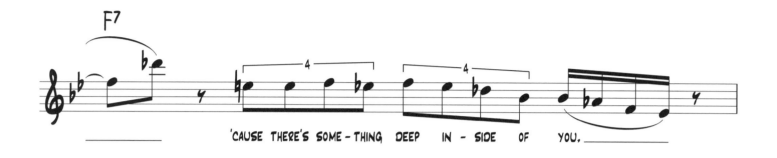

Additional Lyrics

2. You just love that woman so much it's a shame and a sin.
   Yes, you just love that woman so much it's a shame and a sin.
   Yes, you know, yes, you know she belongs to your very best friend.

3. Yes, have you evere loved a woman, one that you know you can't leave alone?
   Yes, have you evere loved a woman, yeah, one that you know you can't leave alone?
   Yes, 'cause there's something deep inside of you, won't let you wreck your best friend's home.

As the Years Go Passing By

Words and Music by Deadric Malone

3RD TIME, TO CODA

AS THE YEARS ___ GO PASS - IN' BY. _____

2. I GIVE YOU

SOLOS

D.S. AL CODA

3. I'M GON-NA

CODA

BY. _____

ADDITIONAL LYRICS

2. I GIVE YOU ALL I OWN; THAT'S ONE THING YOU CAN'T DENY.
    YEAH, I GIVE YOU ALL I OWN; YOU KNOW THAT'S ONE THING YOU CAN'T DENY.
    YES, MY LOVE WILL FOLLOW YOU AS THE YEARS GO PASSING BY.

3. I'M GONNA LEAVE IT UP TO YOU. SO LONG, SO LONG GOODBYE.
    I'M GONNA LEAVE IT UP TO YOU. SO LONG, SO LONG GOODBYE.
    YOU KNOW, MY LOVE WILL FOLLOW YOU AS THE YEARS GO PASSING BY.

Darlin' You Know I Love You

Words and Music by B.B. King and Jules Bihari

HOLD YOU IN MY ARMS TO - NIGHT. 3. OH,

SOLOS

OUTRO-VERSE

OH, DAR-LIN', YOU KNOW I LOVE YOU AND

LOVE YOU BY MY - SELF, BUT YOU'VE GONE AND

LEFT ME, BA - BY, FOR SOME-ONE ELSE.

ADDITIONAL LYRICS

2. I THINK OF YOU EV'RY MORNING
AND DREAM OF YOU EV'RY NIGHT.
AND I WOULD LOVE TO BE WITH YOU ALWAYS.

3. OH, DARLIN', YOU KNOW I LOVE YOU
AND LOVE YOU BY MYSELF,
BUT YOU'VE GONE AND LEFT ME FOR SOMEONE ELSE.

I'd Rather Go Blind

Words and Music by Ellington Jordan and Billy Foster

CD TRACK

6 Full Stereo Mix

14 Split Mix

E♭ Version

Somebody Loan Me a Dime

Words and Music by Fenton Robinson

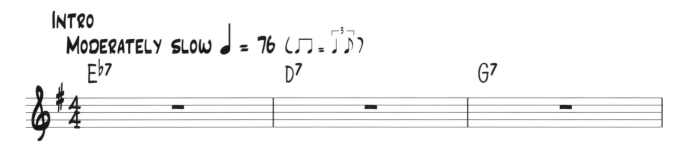

INTRO
Moderately slow ♩ = 76

E♭7　　D7　　G7

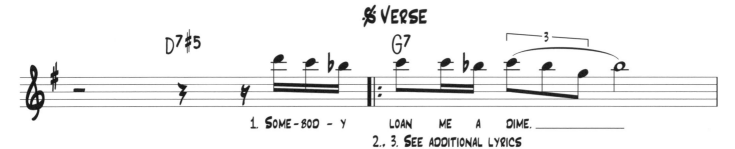

% VERSE

D7♯5　　G7

1. Some-bod - y loan me a dime. _____
2., 3. See additional lyrics

C9　　G7

I wan - na call _____ my old - time used to be. _____

C9

Some-bod - y loan me a dime _____ I tell you. _____

G7

I wan - na call my old-time used to be. _____

3rd Time, To Coda ⊕

E♭7

You know the wom - an she been gone so long, _____

AND, NOW, I'VE BE - GAN _____ TO WOR - RY ME. _____

2. NOW I JUST

SOLOS

D.S. AL CODA

3. AND NOW I

CODA

JUST TO EASE __ MY WOR-RIED MIND. ___

ADDITIONAL LYRICS

2. NOW, I JUST CRY, I JUST CRY, I CRY LIKE A BABY ALL NIGHT LONG.
OH, HOW I CRY, HOW I CRY, I CRY LIKE A BABY ALL NIGHT LONG.
BUT OH, I NEED SOMEBODY, I NEED SOMEBODY HERE IN MY HOME.

3. AND NOW I KNOW SHE'S A GOOD GIRL, BUT AT THAT TIME I JUST DIDN'T UNDERSTAND.
OH, I KNOW, I KNOW SHE'S A GOOD GIRL, BUT AT THAT TIME I JUST DIDN'T UNDERSTAND.
BUT OH, SOMEBODY LOAN ME A DIME, JUST TO EASE MY WORRIED MIND.

Third Degree

Written by Willie Dixon and Eddie Boyd

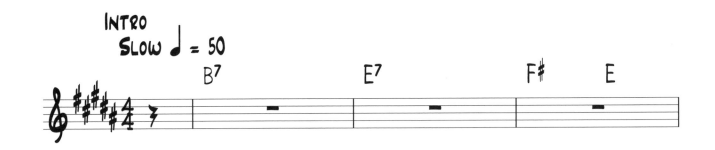

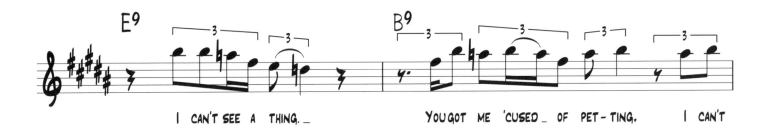

1. Got me 'cused of peep-ing.
2., 3. See additional lyrics

I can't see a thing.___ You got me 'cused of pet-ting, I can't

E-ven raise my hand._____ Bad luck,_____

Bad___ luck is kill-in' me. Now, I

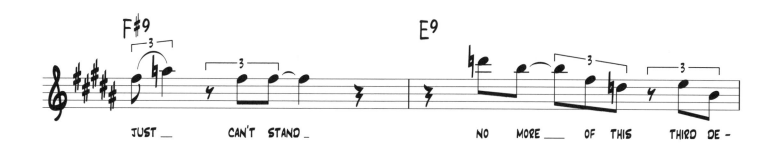

JUST ___ CAN'T STAND ___ NO MORE ___ OF THIS THIRD DE -

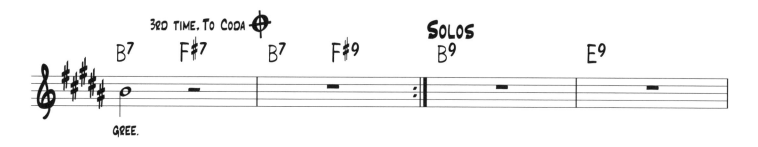

3RD TIME. TO CODA ⊕

SOLOS

GREE.

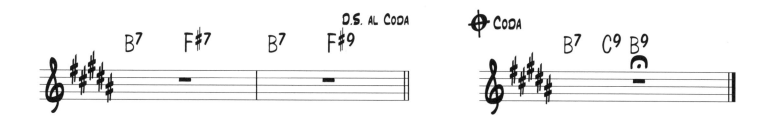

D.S. AL CODA

⊕ CODA

ADDITIONAL LYRICS

2. GOT ME 'CUSED OF MURDER. I'VE NEVER HARMED A MAN.
   YOU GOT ME 'CUSED OF FORGERY, I CAN'T EVEN WRITE MY NAME.
   BAD LUCK, BAD LUCK IS KILLIN' ME.
   NOW, I JUST CAN'T STAND NO MORE OF THIS THIRD DEGREE.

3. GOT ME 'CUSED OF TAXES, I DON'T HAVE A LOUSY DIME.
   YOU GOT ME 'CUSED OF CHILDREN, AIN'T NARY ONE OF THEM MINE.
   BAD LUCK, BAD LUCK IS KILLIN' ME.
   NOW, I JUST CAN'T STAND NO MORE OF THIS THIRD DEGREE.

Three Hours Past Midnight

Words and Music by Johnny Watson and Saul Bihari

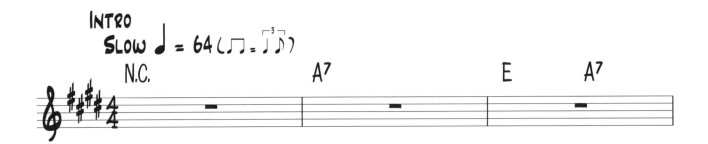

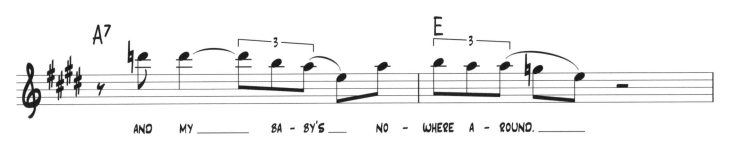

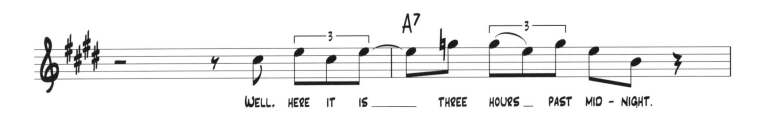

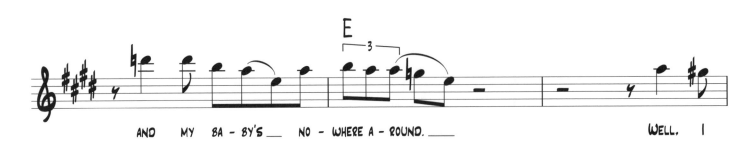

Additional Lyrics

2. Yes, I tossed and tumbled on my pillow, but I just can't close my eyes.
   Yes, I tossed and tumbled on my pillow, and I just can't close my eyes.
   If my baby don't come back pretty quick,
   Yes, I just can't be satisfied.

3. Well, I want my baby, I want her by my side.
   Well, I want my baby, yes, I want her by my side.
   Well, and if she don't come home pretty soon,
   Yes, I just can't be satisfied.

Ain't No Sunshine
Words and Music by Bill Withers

Intro
Moderately slow ♩ = 78

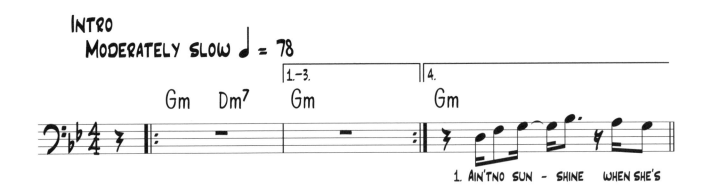

1. Ain't no sun - shine when she's

Verse

gone.
2. See additional lyrics

It's not warm ___ when ___ she's a -

way.   Ain't no sun - shine ___ when she's

Dm⁷   Cm⁷

gone. ___ she's al - ways gone ___ too long   an - y - time she goes a -

way.   2. I won - der this ___ time where she's

I KNOW, I KNOW, I KNOW.

I KNOW, I KNOW, I KNOW. I KNOW, I KNOW, I KNOW.

I KNOW, I KNOW, I KNOW. I OUGHT TO LEAVE THE YOUNG THING A - LONE 'CAUSE AIN'T NO SUN -

- SHINE WHEN SHE'S GONE.

VERSE

3. AIN'T NO SUN - SHINE WHEN SHE'S GONE.
4. SEE ADDITIONAL LYRICS

ON - LY DARK - NESS EV - 'RY DAY.

AIN'T NO SUN - SHINE WHEN SHE'S GONE, SHE'S AL - WAYS GONE TOO

LONG, AN - Y - TIME SHE GOES A - WAY.

AN - Y - TIME ___ SHE GOES A - WAY.

AN - Y - TIME ___ SHE GOES A -

Additional Lyrics

2. I wonder this time where she's gone,
I wonder if she's gone to stay.
Ain't no sunshine when she's gone,
And this house just ain't no home.
Anytime she goes away.

4. It's not warm when she's away,
Only darkness every day.
Ain't no sunshine when she's gone,
She's always gone too long,
Anytime she goes away.

Have You Ever Loved a Woman

Words and Music by Billy Myles

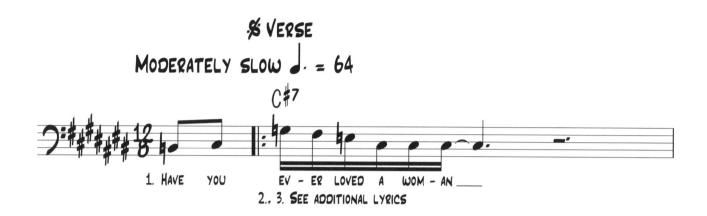

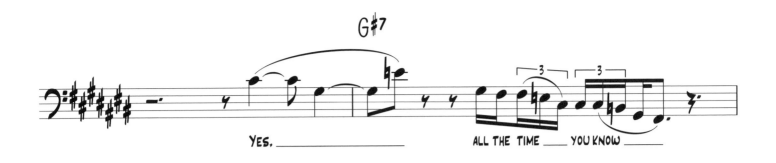

YES, _____ ALL THE TIME ____ YOU KNOW ____

SHE ___ BEARS ___ AN - OTH - ER MAN'S _____ NAME. _____

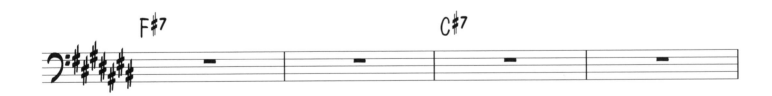

2. YOU JUST

SOLOS

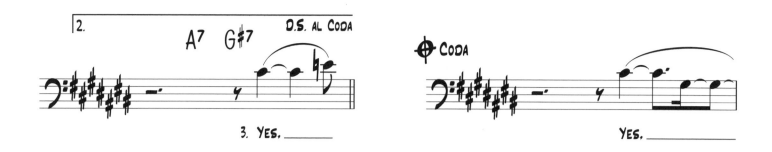

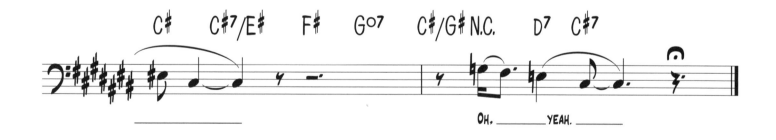

Additional Lyrics

2. You just love that woman so much it's a shame and a sin.
   Yes, you just love that woman so much it's a shame and a sin.
   Yes, you know, yes, you know she belongs to your very best friend.

3. Yes, have you evere loved a woman, one that you know you can't leave alone?
   Yes, have you evere loved a woman, yeah, one that you know you can't leave alone?
   Yes, 'cause there's something deep inside of you, won't let you wreck your best friend's home.

As the Years Go Passing By

Words and Music by Deadric Malone

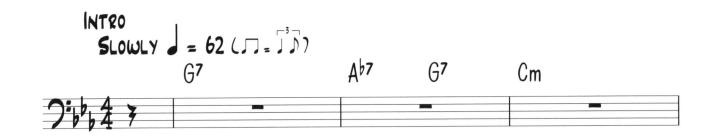

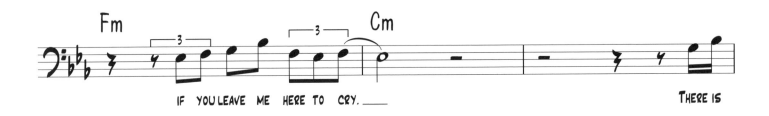

Additional Lyrics

2. I give you all I own; that's one thing you can't deny.
   Yeah, I give you all I own; you know that's one thing you can't deny.
   Yes, my love will follow you as the years go passing by.

3. I'm gonna leave it up to you. So long, so long goodbye.
   I'm gonna leave it up to you. So long, so long goodbye.
   You know, my love will follow you as the years go passing by.

Darlin' You Know I Love You

Words and Music by B.B. King and Jules Bihari

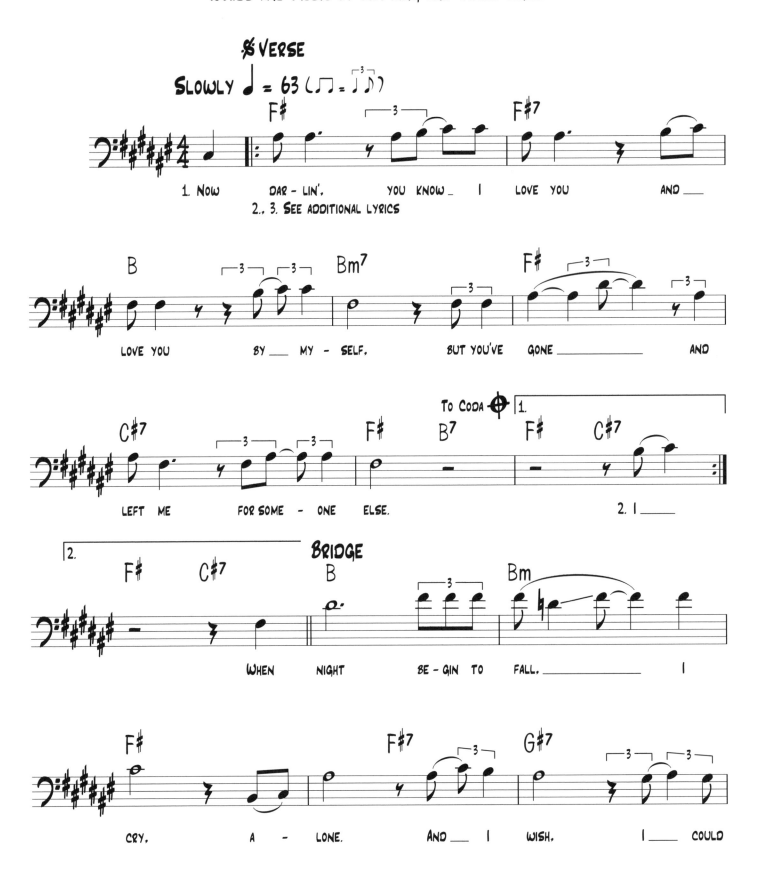

5 FULL STEREO MIX
13 SPLIT MIX

𝄢 C VERSION

I'd Rather Go Blind

WORDS AND MUSIC BY ELLINGTON JORDAN AND BILLY FOSTER

INTRO
SLOW ♩. = 55

VERSE

1. Some-thing told ___ me it was o-ver when I saw ___ you ___ and her talk-ing. ___ Some-thing deep down in my soul ___ said, "Cry, ___ girl," ___ when I saw you ___ and that girl ___ walk-ing. ___ now.

CHORUS

I would rath-er, I would rath-er go blind, ___ boy, ___ than to see you walk a-way ___ from me, child. ___ 2. Oo, ___

VERSE

So you see, I love you so much that I don't wan-na watch you leave me, ba-by.

Somebody Loan Me a Dime

Words and Music by Fenton Robinson

Intro
Moderately slow ♩ = 76

1. Some-bod - y loan me a dime. _____
2., 3. See additional lyrics

I wan - na call _____ my old - time used to be. _____

Some-bod - y loan me a dime _____ I tell you. _____

I wan - na call my old-time used to be. _____

You know the wom - an she been gone so long, _____

AND, NOW, I'VE BE- GAN _____ TO WOR - RY ME. _____

2. NOW I JUST

JUST TO EASE _ MY WOR-RIED MIND. __

ADDITIONAL LYRICS

2. NOW, I JUST CRY, I JUST CRY, I CRY LIKE A BABY ALL NIGHT LONG.
   OH, HOW I CRY, HOW I CRY, I CRY LIKE A BABY ALL NIGHT LONG.
   BUT OH, I NEED SOMEBODY, I NEED SOMEBODY HERE IN MY HOME.

3. AND NOW I KNOW SHE'S A GOOD GIRL, BUT AT THAT TIME I JUST DIDN'T UNDERSTAND.
   OH, I KNOW, I KNOW SHE'S A GOOD GIRL, BUT AT THAT TIME I JUST DIDN'T UNDERSTAND.
   BUT OH, SOMEBODY LOAN ME A DIME, JUST TO EASE MY WORRIED MIND.

Third Degree
Written by Willie Dixon and Eddie Boyd

INTRO
SLOW ♩ = 50

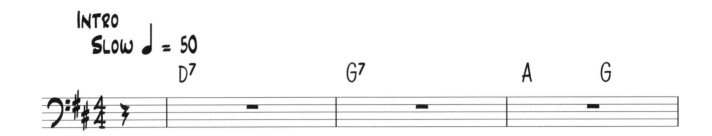

1. Got me 'cused of peep - ing.
2., 3. See additional lyrics

I can't see a thing. ___   You got me 'cused of pet - ting.   I can't

E - ven raise my hand. ___   Bad   luck, ___

Bad ___ luck   is kill - in' me.   Now, I

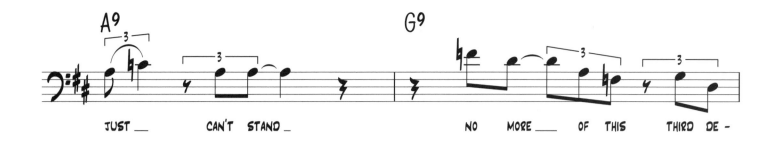

JUST __ CAN'T STAND __ NO MORE __ OF THIS THIRD DE -

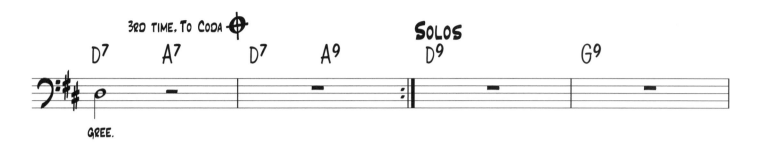

GREE.

Additional Lyrics

2. Got me 'cused of murder, I've never harmed a man.
   You got me 'cused of forgery, I can't even write my name.
   Bad luck, bad luck is killin' me.
   Now, I just can't stand no more of this third degree.

3. Got me 'cused of taxes, I don't have a lousy dime.
   You got me 'cused of children, ain't nary one of them mine.
   Bad luck, bad luck is killin' me.
   Now, I just can't stand no more of this third degree.

Three Hours Past Midnight
Words and Music by Johnny Watson and Saul Bihari

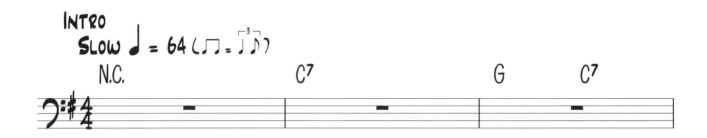

1. Well, here is it _____ three hours _ past mid - night.
2., 3. See additional lyrics

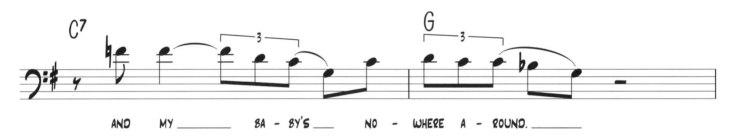

and my _____ ba - by's _ no - where a - round. _____

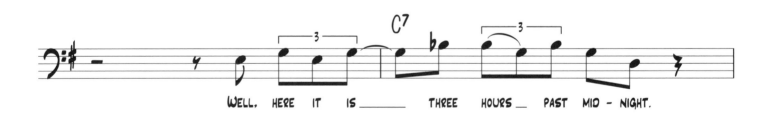

Well, here it is _____ three hours _ past mid - night.

and my ba - by's _ no - where a - round. ___ Well, I

LIS-TEN SO HARD ___ TO HEAR HER FOOT-STEPS,   AN' I AIN'T E - VEN _____

HEARD A SOUND. _   2. YES,

SOLOS

3. WELL,   FIED.

Additional Lyrics

2. YES, I TOSSED AND TUMBLED ON MY PILLOW, BUT I JUST CAN'T CLOSE MY EYES.
   YES, I TOSSED AND TUMBLED ON MY PILLOW, AND I JUST CAN'T CLOSE MY EYES.
   IF MY BABY DON'T COME BACK PRETTY QUICK,
   YES, I JUST CAN'T BE SATISFIED.

3. WELL, I WANT MY BABY, I WANT HER BY MY SIDE.
   WELL, I WANT MY BABY, YES, I WANT HER BY MY SIDE.
   WELL, AND IF SHE DON'T COME HOME PRETTY SOON,
   YES, I JUST CAN'T BE SATISFIED.

The Best-Selling Jazz Book of All Time Is Now Legal!

The Real Books are the most popular jazz books of all time. Since the 1970s, musicians have trusted these volumes to get them through every gig, night after night. The problem is that the books were illegally produced and distributed, without any regard to copyright law, or royalties paid to the composers who created these musical masterpieces.

Hal Leonard is very proud to present the first legitimate and legal editions of these books ever produced. You won't even notice the difference, other than all the notorious errors being fixed: the covers and typeface look the same, the song lists are nearly identical, and the price for our edition is even cheaper than the originals!

Every conscientious musician will appreciate that these books are now produced accurately and ethically, benefitting the songwriters that we owe for some of the greatest tunes of all time!

Also available:

00240264	The Real Blues Book	$34.99
00310910	The Real Bluegrass Book	$29.99
00240440	The Trane Book	$22.99
00240137	Miles Davis Real Book	$19.95
00240355	The Real Dixieland Book	$29.99
00122335	The Real Dixieland Book B♭ Edition	$29.99
00240235	The Duke Ellington Real Book	$19.99
00240268	The Real Jazz Solos Book	$30.00
00240348	The Real Latin Book	$35.00
00127107	The Real Latin Book B♭ Edition	$35.00
00240358	The Charlie Parker Real Book	$19.99
00240331	The Bud Powell Real Book	$19.99
00240437	The Real R&B Book	$39.99
00240313	The Real Rock Book	$35.00
00240323	The Real Rock Book – Vol. 2	$35.00
00240359	The Real Tab Book	$32.50
00240317	The Real Worship Book	$29.99

VOLUME 1

00240221	C Edition	$35.00
00240224	B♭ Edition	$35.00
00240225	E♭ Edition	$35.00
00240226	Bass Clef Edition	$35.00
00240292	C Edition 6 x 9	$30.00
00240339	B♭ Edition 6 x 9	$30.00
00451087	C Edition on CD-ROM	$25.00
00240302	A-D CD Backing Tracks	$24.99
00240303	E-J CD Backing Tracks	$24.95
00240304	L-R CD Backing Tracks	$24.95
00240305	S-Z CD Backing Tracks	$24.99
00110604	Book/USB Flash Drive Backing Tracks Pack	$79.99
00110599	USB Flash Drive Only	$50.00

VOLUME 2

00240222	C Edition	$35.50
00240227	B♭ Edition	$35.00
00240228	E♭ Edition	$35.00
00240229	Bass Clef Edition	$35.00
00240293	C Edition 6 x 9	$30.00
00125900	B♭ Edition 6 x 9	$30.00
00451088	C Edition on CD-ROM	$27.99
00240351	A-D CD Backing Tracks	$24.99
00240352	E-I CD Backing Tracks	$24.99
00240353	J-R CD Backing Tracks	$24.99
00240354	S-Z CD Backing Tracks	$24.99

THE REAL CHRISTMAS BOOK

00240306	C Edition	$29.99
00240345	B♭ Edition	$29.99
00240346	E♭ Edition	$29.99
00240347	Bass Clef Edition	$29.99
00240431	A-G CD Backing Tracks	$24.99
00240432	H-M CD Backing Tracks	$24.99
00240433	N-Y CD Backing Tracks	$24.99

THE REAL VOCAL BOOK

00240230	Volume 1 High Voice	$35.00
00240307	Volume 1 Low Voice	$35.00
00240231	Volume 2 High Voice	$35.00
00240308	Volume 2 Low Voice	$35.00
00240391	Volume 3 High Voice	$35.00
00240392	Volume 3 Low Voice	$35.00
00118318	Volume 4 High Voice	$35.00
00118319	Volume 4 Low Voice	$35.00

VOLUME 3

00240233	C Edition	$35.00
00240284	B♭ Edition	$35.00
00240285	E♭ Edition	$35.00
00240286	Bass Clef Edition	$35.00
00240338	C Edition 6 x 9	$30.00
00451089	C Edition on CD-ROM	$29.99

THE REAL BOOK – STAFF PAPER

00240327		$10.99

HOW TO PLAY FROM A REAL BOOK
For All Musicians
by Robert Rawlins

00312097		$17.50

VOLUME 4

00240296	C Edition	$35.00
00103348	B♭ Edition	$35.00
00103349	E♭ Edition	$35.00
00103350	Bass Clef Edition	$35.00

VOLUME 5

00240349	C Edition	$35.00

Complete song lists online at www.halleonard.com
Prices, content, and availability subject to change without notice.

HAL•LEONARD®
CORPORATION
7777 W. Bluemound Rd. P.O. Box 13819 Milwaukee, WI 53213

1214

ARTIST TRANSCRIPTIONS®

Artist Transcriptions are authentic, note-for-note transcriptions of today's hottest artists in jazz, pop and rock. These outstanding, accurate arrangements are in an easy-to-read format which includes all essential lines. **Artist Transcriptions** can be used to perform, sequence or for reference.

CLARINET

00672423	Buddy De Franco Collection	$19.95

FLUTE

00672379	Eric Dolphy Collection	$19.95
00672582	The Very Best of James Galway	$16.99
00672372	James Moody Collection – Sax and Flute	$19.95

GUITAR & BASS

00660113	The Guitar Style of George Benson	$14.95
00699072	Guitar Book of Pierre Bensusan	$29.95
00672331	Ron Carter – Acoustic Bass	$16.95
00672307	Stanley Clarke Collection	$19.95
00660115	Al Di Meola – Friday Night in San Francisco	$14.95
00604043	Al Di Meola – Music, Words, Pictures	$14.95
00672574	Al Di Meola – Pursuit of Radical Rhapsody	$22.99
00673245	Jazz Style of Tal Farlow	$19.95
00699306	Jim Hall – Exploring Jazz Guitar	$19.95
00604049	Allan Holdsworth – Reaching for the Uncommon Chord	$14.95
00699215	Leo Kottke – Eight Songs	$14.95
00675536	Wes Montgomery – Guitar Transcriptions	$17.95
00672353	Joe Pass Collection	$18.95
00673216	John Patitucci	$16.95
00027083	Django Reinhardt Antholog	$14.95
00026711	Genius of Django Reinhardt	$10.95
00672374	Johnny Smith Guitar Solos	$19.99

PIANO & KEYBOARD

00672338	Monty Alexander Collection	$19.95
00672487	Monty Alexander Plays Standards	$19.95
00672520	Count Basie Collection	$19.95
00672439	Cyrus Chestnut Collection	$19.95
00672300	Chick Corea – Paint the World	$12.95
14037739	Storyville Presents Duke Ellington	$19.99
00672537	Bill Evans at Town Hall	$16.95
00672548	The Mastery of Bill Evans	$12.95
00672425	Bill Evans – Piano Interpretations	$19.95
00672365	Bill Evans – Piano Standards	$19.95
00672510	Bill Evans Trio – Vol. 1: 1959-1961	$24.95
00672511	Bill Evans Trio – Vol. 2: 1962-1965	$24.95
00672512	Bill Evans Trio – Vol. 3: 1968-1974	$24.95
00672513	Bill Evans Trio – Vol. 4: 1979-1980	$24.95
00672381	Tommy Flanagan Collection	$24.99
00672492	Benny Goodman Collection	$16.95
00672486	Vince Guaraldi Collection	$19.95
00672419	Herbie Hancock Collection	$19.95
00672438	Hampton Hawes	$19.95
14037738	Storyville Presents Earl Hines	$19.99
00672322	Ahmad Jamal Collection	$22.95
00672564	Best of Jeff Lorber	$17.99
00672476	Brad Mehldau Collection	$19.99
00672388	Best of Thelonious Monk	$19.95
00672389	Thelonious Monk Collection	$19.95

00672390	Thelonious Monk Plays Jazz Standards – Volume 1	$19.95
00672391	Thelonious Monk Plays Jazz Standards – Volume 2	$19.95
00672433	Jelly Roll Morton – The Piano Rolls	$12.95
00672553	Charlie Parker for Piano	$19.95
00672542	Oscar Peterson – Jazz Piano Solos	$16.95
00672562	Oscar Peterson – A Jazz Portrait of Frank Sinatra	$19.95
00672544	Oscar Peterson – Originals	$9.95
00672532	Oscar Peterson – Plays Broadway	$19.95
00672531	Oscar Peterson – Plays Duke Ellington	$19.95
00672563	Oscar Peterson – A Royal Wedding Suite	$19.99
00672533	Oscar Peterson – Trios	$24.95
00672543	Oscar Peterson Trio – Canadiana Suite	$10.99
00672534	Very Best of Oscar Peterson	$22.95
00672371	Bud Powell Classics	$19.95
00672376	Bud Powell Collection	$19.95
00672507	Gonzalo Rubalcaba Collection	$19.95
00672303	Horace Silver Collection	$19.95
00672316	Art Tatum Collection	$22.95
00672355	Art Tatum Solo Book	$19.95
00672357	Billy Taylor Collection	$24.95
00673215	McCoy Tyner	$16.95
00672321	Cedar Walton Collection	$19.95
00672519	Kenny Werner Collection	$19.95
00672434	Teddy Wilson Collection	$19.95
14037740	Storyville Presents Teddy Wilson	$19.99

SAXOPHONE

00672566	The Mindi Abair Collection	$14.99
00673244	Julian "Cannonball" Adderley Collection	$19.95
00673237	Michael Brecker	$19.95
00672429	Michael Brecker Collection	$19.95
00672315	Benny Carter Plays Standards	$22.95
00672394	James Carter Collection	$19.95
00672349	John Coltrane Plays Giant Steps	$19.95
00672529	John Coltrane – Giant Steps	$14.99
00672494	John Coltrane – A Love Supreme	$14.95
00307393	John Coltrane – Omnibook: C Instruments	$24.99
00307391	John Coltrane – Omnibook: B-flat Instruments	$19.99
00307392	John Coltrane – Omnibook: E-flat Instruments	$24.99
00307394	John Coltrane – Omnibook: Bass Clef Instruments	$24.99
00672493	John Coltrane Plays "Coltrane Changes"	$19.95
00672453	John Coltrane Plays Standards	$19.95
00673233	John Coltrane Solos	$22.95
00672328	Paul Desmond Collection	$19.95
00672379	Eric Dolphy Collection	$19.95
00672530	Kenny Garrett Collection	$19.95
00699375	Stan Getz	$19.95

00672377	Stan Getz – Bossa Novas	$19.95
00672375	Stan Getz – Standards	$18.95
00673254	Great Tenor Sax Solos	$18.95
00672523	Coleman Hawkins Collection	$19.95
00673252	Joe Henderson – Selections from "Lush Life" & "So Near So Far"	$19.95
00672330	Best of Joe Henderson	$22.95
00672350	Tenor Saxophone Standards	$18.95
00673239	Best of Kenny G	$19.95
00673229	Kenny G – Breathless	$19.95
00672462	Kenny G – Classics in the Key of G	$19.95
00672485	Kenny G – Faith: A Holiday Album	$14.95
00672373	Kenny G – The Moment	$19.95
00672326	Joe Lovano Collection	$19.95
00672498	Jackie McLean Collection	$19.95
00672372	James Moody Collection – Sax and Flute	$19.95
00672416	Frank Morgan Collection	$19.95
00672539	Gerry Mulligan Collection	$19.95
00672352	Charlie Parker Collection	$19.95
00672561	Best of Sonny Rollins	$19.95
00672444	Sonny Rollins Collection	$19.95
00102751	Sonny Rollins with the Modern Jazz Quartet	$17.99
00675000	David Sanborn Collection	$17.95
00672528	Bud Shank Collection	$19.95
00672491	New Best of Wayne Shorter	$19.95
00672550	The Sonny Stitt Collection	$19.95
00672350	Tenor Saxophone Standards	$18.95
00672567	The Best of Kim Waters	$17.99
00672524	Lester Young Collection	$19.95

TROMBONE

00672332	J.J. Johnson Collection	$19.95
00672489	Steve Turré Collection	$19.99

TRUMPET

00672557	Herb Alpert Collection	$14.99
00672480	Louis Armstrong Collection	$17.95
00672481	Louis Armstrong Plays Standards	$17.95
00672435	Chet Baker Collection	$19.95
00672556	Best of Chris Botti	$19.95
00672448	Miles Davis – Originals, Vol. 1	$19.95
00672451	Miles Davis – Originals, Vol. 2	$19.95
00672450	Miles Davis – Standards, Vol. 1	$19.95
00672449	Miles Davis – Standards, Vol. 2	$19.95
00672479	Dizzy Gillespie Collection	$19.95
00673214	Freddie Hubbard	$14.95
00672382	Tom Harrell – Jazz Trumpet	$19.95
00672363	Jazz Trumpet Solos	$9.95
00672506	Chuck Mangione Collection	$19.95
00672525	Arturo Sandoval – Trumpet Evolution	$19.95

HAL•LEONARD®
CORPORATION

7777 W. BLUEMOUND RD. P.O. BOX 13819 MILWAUKEE, WI 53213

Visit our web site for a complete listing of our titles with songlists at

www.halleonard.com

0913

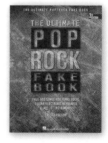